3 TO A SESSION:
A MONSTER'S
TALE
&
LAZARUS
DISPOSED

Desi Moreno-Penson

BROADWAY PLAY PUBLISHING INC
New York
www.broadwayplaypublishing.com
info@broadwayplaypublishing.com

First printing: December 2011
I S B N: 978-0-88145-516-8

Book design: Marie Donovan
Page make-up: Adobe Indesign
Typeface: Palatino

ABOUT THE AUTHOR

Desi Moreno-Penson: Is a playwright and actress based in N Y C. Her play, DEVIL LAND, was selected for the 4th Annual Summer Play Festival produced by Arielle Tepper Madover. Other productions include GHOST LIGHT at 59E59 Theatre, and 3 TO A SESSION: A MONSTER'S TALE which won Best Play at the 2005 Downtown Urban Theater Festival at the Cherry Lane, and was part of the 2004 New Works Lab at INTAR. Solo performance pieces, A LATINA PREPARES and DON'T KNOCK IT 'TIL YOU TRY IT, have been presented in such venues as The Henry Street Settlement and The Bronx Academy of Arts and Dance (BAAD). Her short plays, SPIRIT SEX and COMIDA DE PUTA (F@%KING LOUSY FOOD), have been presented as part of the Going to the River Festival at The Ensemble Studio Theater and SPIRIT SEX was selected for the short plays anthology published by Smith and Kraus, *2010: The Best Ten-Minute Plays*. Another short play, LAZARUS DISPOSED, was selected for production at the 14th Annual International Women's Playwriting Festival at Perishable Theatre in Providence, RI. Desi is a finalist for the 2007 Princess Grace Fellowship for emerging artists, a three-time grant recipient of the BRIO (Bronx Recognizes Its Own) Playwriting/Performance Fellowships sponsored by The Bronx Council on the Arts, The 2002 Louis Delgado Jr Playwriting Award, and is a finalist winner for the 2002-2003 New Voices Playwriting Competition at Repertorio Espanol for her play, BEIGE. As an actress, she has performed at Urban Stages, The Puerto Rican Traveling Theater, Hospital Audiences, Inc, The Cherry Lane, Jean Cocteau Repertory, The Nuyorican Poets Café, Studio Arena Theater in Buffalo, as well as The Royal Court Theatre in London, and she has appeared in such films as Spike Lee's *Girl 6*, and *Extreme Measures* with Hugh Grant. She is a member of The Screen Actors Guild, The Dramatists Guild, and has been a member of The Professional Playwrights Unit at The Puerto Rican Traveling Theater and The Hispanic Playwrights Residence Lab (H P R L) at INTAR. She holds a Master's Degree in Dramaturgy and Theater/ Literary Criticism from Brooklyn College where she received the prestigious Samuel Levenson Memorial Scholarship for academic and creative achievement. Desi is represented by Bruce Ostler at Bret Adams, Ltd.

3 TO A SESSION: A MONSTER'S TALE

3 TO A SESSION: A MONSTER'S TALE was first produced as part of the 2005 Downtown Urban Theater Festival (Producing Director, Marc Newell; Executive Director, Roy Cosme) at The Cherry Lane Theater (Producing Artistic Director, Angelina Fiordellisi) in New York City on 22 June 2005. The cast and creative contributors were:

ALLY ....Desi Moreno-Penson
PAULA...Arlene Chico-Lugo
VINCENT ....Phillip Boyle

Director ....Jose Zayas
Theater technician...Sarah Bell
Stage manager...Dirk Smile
Sound designer..David M Lawson

CHARACTERS & SETTING

ALLY, 30s-40s. *She likes to read books, is usually the "patient" and the "lesbian". Smart, more of a steely-eyed realist than anyone else. Might or might not be* VINCENT's *mother, Alicia.*

PAULA, 20s-30s. *She LOVES plants and loves to be right. Easily frightened. Usually plays the uptight "psychiatrist". Has beautiful long, dark hair. Might or might not be* VINCENT's *Titi Paola.*

VINCENT, *early 30s-40s. He controls this space. Is introspective, bombastic, and child-like, and at times, playful and thoughtful. We don't know with whom he's talking to, not sure if he knows either.*

Time and Place: A room that can only be found in one's imagination. A limbotic place. A surreal consigned resting place only to be found in the Theatre of the Absurd.

Playwright's note: Although the Scenic Designer should be encouraged to play creatively with the idea of a minimal set, with the emphasis being primarily on the actors and text, another way to go can be with the sofa chair, lamp, plants, and chest of drawers all having a cartoonish look and feel to it. Either oversized, and/or painted in bright Crayola colors. Ideally, it should have a Pee-Wee's Playhouse kind of impression and feel. Just a thought.

I am only what I create. All that exists, exists only in my awareness.
Alexander Scriabin

The world is a reflection of your interior state.
August Strindberg

But a threatening shadow follows me everywhere,
And I do not know when I shall be freed from this darkness.
Perhaps only by God's deliverance.
Tadeusz Micinski

I believe only in what I do not see.
Gustave Moreau

(The stage is in blackout. We hear the combined sounds of what seems to be that of a Frankenstein monster and the sounds of a woman about to reach orgasm. These noises continue to progress and build until they finally reach a crescendo. At this point, lights come up on a room. To the left there is a door, a bookcase filled with books in a decidedly disheveled manner. More books all strewn around. There are also Hustler and Playboy magazines thrown around the floor as well. To the rear, a pitcher of orange juice on a chest of drawers. To the left of the stage, a bunch of green plants, some of them thriving, others are dying. There is a spot on VINCENT *who is dressed as a hospital orderly. The rest of the stage remains in blackout. He addresses the audience.)*

VINCENT: My father lay down with bitches. He was proud of it.
He used to say, "Hey, you want to be seen as a man?
Then you gotta fuck...
'Cause that's what a man does...
And as often as he can...
With as many women as he can...
Because that's what it means to be a man...
A man...CAN..."
I wasn't good. At understanding that. The *can* of it.
I couldn't understand why my Moms wasn't enough.
But she wasn't.
My Pops used to say that he couldn't do *certain* things with *Mami*
That he could do with bought bitches...
He'd say that if the Italians and Jamaicans in the neighborhood could understand that

Then why couldn't his own son?
He called me a *maricon*…
He'd accuse me of wanting to fuck my own mother.
You know, like in *Oedipus Rex*…
Kill the father and marry the mother…
I'd call him an asshole.
And then he'd strike me in the face with his belt
buckle. Or his fist. Or his boot.
I hated him. Him and his bitches. But sometimes, I
hated the bitches even more.
Because I knew that if they hadn't been around, then
Papi couldn't cheat on my Moms.
So, it was their fault—for always being there. You
know? Always showing him their *cositas*.
And mami knew, you know?
Ella no era estupida…
Ella era una espiritista…
She was a spiritualist, *tu sabes?* She could have visions.
She always knew about everything that was going on
in that house. And in our heads. Our souls… *Ella era
una santa; una estrella, una poder divina…*
With her jet-black eyes and nut-brown skin…
She was so strong and beautiful…so smart…
But they fought a lot. He smashed a beer bottle in her
face one time.
Mami called him a monster.
"Ese mo'tro; ese jodia hombre me ba matar…!" she'd say.
So she spent all of her time with her friend, *Titi Paola*.
No, she wasn't really my *Titi*.
But she liked it when I called her that.
Titi Paola… She was beautiful, too.
The two of them knew each other from the public
school
Where they worked…
My Dad didn't work. On account of his bad back. At
least that was his excuse.

So my moms was tired a lot.
And when she'd leave for the day that was my Dad's
cue.
And then he'd bring them home.
The bitches.
So many bitches…
So little time…

(Blackout on VINCENT. *There is an immediate spot on* ALLY.
*She holds a book in her lap. She addresses the audience. She
is agitated and begins to wring her hands.)*

ALLY: I don't have much time. So I'm going to tell you
what I know.
We couldn't stick to a session. No matter how much we
tried.
And we really did try. But after awhile, it got
impossible.
No one would listen to each other. *No one.*

(There is a spot on PAULA. *She is standing among the plants
with a watering can in her hands. She is also noticeably
nervous and ill at ease. She keeps trying to water the plants
but her hands are visibly shaking.)*

PAULA: There was never any reason to change. Why
bother?
We knew what we had to do. We weren't supposed to
keep
Interrupting the session. Every now and then, okay—
But not *every five minutes!* We were asking for trouble.
And trouble was something we couldn't afford.
Not here anyway.

ALLY: It was easier without memory. *That's* what did
us in.
You could keep to the session without memory.

But with it—it was impossible.

PAULA: It wasn't impossible—

ALLY: *(Turning towards her; angrily)* Yes, it was! How can you say that when you've seen what's happened?

PAULA: *(Overlapping on her second line; rapidly, not looking at her)* Don't speak to me! If you speak to me, they'll start up again and *it* will come back—

ALLY: *(Looking away from* PAULA; *fearfully)* I'm sorry. I'm sorry. I forgot myself.

(A beat. PAULA *tries to water the plants again, and then sets down the can. She remains motionless, staring straight ahead of her.* ALLY *is pretending to read.)*

PAULA: *(Not moving, not looking at her)* Why is it here?

ALLY: I don't know. *(A pause)* Don't speak to me.

(A beat. The two women remain in stony silence. ALLY *attempts to read her book;* PAULA *attempts to water her plants. It doesn't work. After a few more moments,* ALLY *turns to address the audience again.)*

ALLY: *(Loud, frantic whisper)* The last time I was this frightened I was little. Okay, maybe not so little. Maybe I was thirty-five. Actually, I don't remember how old I was. But my husband was drunk on beer. And he could be *vicious* when he was drunk. He insisted that I sit across from him this one time. I don't remember what we talked about. It didn't matter—

PAULA: *(Her attention on a plant; quietly)* Memories don't matter, do they, sweetie? Noooo, they don't—

ALLY: But at one point, he held the beer bottle up…and I knew. I *knew* that any second now it was going to be smashed in my face. All I could do was wait for it. And the whole time, I kept thinking, "What did I do? What horrible things did I do to make you want to smash a beer bottle right into my face, *Papi*?"

PAULA: *(Still on the plant)* I would never hurt my little *snookie-snooks-snooks*—

ALLY: *(With rising anger)* But once I realized that I had in fact, done *nothing*—I could only brace my whole body for the feel of it. For cut glass against my skin. Like a thousand tiny needles forcing my exsanguination. Waiting—without breath. *Como una pendeja!*

PAULA: *(Shaking her watering can)* Oh, *my poor little blossom bundt cake*, no more water for you...! *(A pause)* I hate it when you do that.

ALLY: What?

PAULA: You and your big words. *I'm not your pupil, maestra!*

ALLY: What big words?

PAULA: *(Mimicking her)* "...What big words?" *Ex-sandwich nations*—or whatever you call it. Don't think I didn't notice how you slipped that in there. Do you know what you are?

ALLY: Why don't you tell me?

PAULA: *Tu eres una echona.* You're a little show-off. *(Back to her plants)* I'm not like you. *I know* how to make the best of things.

ALLY: *(Back to the audience)* I wish I could've told my husband to go ahead. I wish I'd had that kind of courage then. To just look him in the face and say, "Go ahead. Go ahead and do it, you sadistic piece of shit and go fuck yourself too, while you're at it." But I was such a coward. My own blood frightened me. And I don't mean the family blood that tied us together. Just the blood that was supposed to be fucking mine to keep...!

PAULA: *(Clipping dead leaves off a plant; to herself)* It's important to know how to adapt. What do you do if you're trapped amongst a pack of wolves?

ALLY: *(To the audience)* You howl your ass off.

PAULA: *(Through clenched teeth)* If you make a comment on what I'm saying, they'll think we're speaking to one another. *Don't speak to me!*

ALLY: *(Turning her head slightly towards* PAULA*)* *You're the one talking to me!* And if you ask a question, you should expect an answer. *(Back to the audience)* I mean that's how it works. It's just like real life.

(Lights up on VINCENT. *He is unseen by* ALLY *and* PAULA. *He addresses the audience again.)*

VINCENT: *(To the audience)* I came home one day after school. And I went into the kitchen to make myself a peanut butter and jelly sandwich. There was a spilled glass of orange juice on the floor. The orange juice was everywhere. That glass must've been filled to the top. Jagged, glistening, shiny bits. All over the kitchen floor. It frightened me. I kept staring at all the shattered glass. Like bright, yellow tears.
And then I pulled out one of the loosies from my pocket. My therapist at the hospital used to say that it was good for me to hold it if it made me feel better. It did. Not 'cause I was going to smoke it or anything. I didn't smoke. It relaxed me to just hold it. And then I heard the monster.

(A horrible sound)

PAULA: Please. I don't want the monster to come back.

ALLY: Even if it does, I don't think it can kill us.

PAULA: *(Shaking her head)* We don't know that. You don't know that.

ALLY: I've got a hunch.

PAULA: No. You're not that smart.

ALLY: Look at the facts. How long have we been here?

PAULA: I don't know. A long time.

ALLY: And since we've been here, what have they threatened us with?

PAULA: *(Searching)* Spiritual—

ALLY: Yes?

PAULA: *(Unsure)* Spiritual…nylons?

ALLY: No. Spiritual *annihilation*. They threaten us with spiritual annihilation. And personally, between you and me, how *bad* does that sound, really?

VINCENT: *(Back to the audience)* I love hearing women talk shit. My Moms and Titi Paola would talk to each other all the time. Of course, I never understood what the hell they were saying. I was too young, I guess. But with things being the way they were with my Dad, she needed a friend like Titi Paola. They were like sisters. Paola was beautiful. Like my moms. She had long hair. Bedroom hair. Sex hair, you know? She worked as a Para with my Moms at the Public School. But she was also a plant nursery worker in Queens.

PAULA: *(Speaking to her plants)* What does that mean? Spiritual annihilation?

ALLY: Does it frighten you?

PAULA: *(Nodding, still not looking at her)* If I knew what it was, I bet I'd be terrified.

ALLY: *(Smile)* I used to think the exact same thing about sex.

VOICEOVER: *(Female voice):* Warning. Twenty seconds to resume session. Or risk spiritual annihilation.

ALLY: *(Yelling back)* We used to have *thirty* seconds, you bitch!

PAULA: You see? You couldn't keep your mouth shut and now look—

ALLY: Oh, come on! I'm not alone in this. How long do you think they were going to let us go without resuming session?

VOICEOVER: 18…17…16…

PAULA: *(Frantic)* Now, we'll be mauled…!

ALLY: *(Also frightened)* As long as we don't open the door, we're fine.

PAULA: For how long? It will eventually knock it down. It will figure out how.

VOICEOVER: 13…12…11…

ALLY: You have to be quiet and let me think!

PAULA: You're the one who can't keep your mouth shut!

ALLY: *(To the audience; rapidly)* The session was always the same…that was the point. A simple scenario; a psychiatrist, a patient, an orderly…

PAULA: STOP TALKING TO THEM!

VOICEOVER: 5…4…3…

ALLY: But that's how we were supposed to keep the monster away. Now that's what they told us. We play out these scenes, these stupid scenes. And we tease, we flirt. *(Laughs)* Like something out of an adult video, you know?

PAULA: But it's always been the three of us…!

VOICEOVER: 1… Resume Session. Line 070. Section 5. Begin.

(A beat. Both PAULA and ALLY gasp out loud and place their hands down to their crotches. Blackout. We hear the sounds of the Frankenstein monster again. As it quickly builds to another crescendo, the lights go up again. We now see PAULA and ALLY "in session". PAULA is looking

through a box of ladies' panties. ALLY *is sitting across from her.)*

PAULA: Which one is yours?

ALLY: They're all mine. All of them.

PAULA: *(Holding up a thong)* Even this?

ALLY: *(Smile)* Especially that one.

PAULA: *(Folds up the thong; tosses it back in the box)* How can anyone wear something that feels so restrictive...so tight...Right up your... *(Embarrassed)*...You know?

ALLY: Up my ass.

PAULA: Yeah. There.

ALLY: Why don't you find out? Put them on.

PAULA: Um...

ALLY: How do you think that would make you feel?

PAULA: *(Out of character)* No...you don't ask that...I ask that... *(Back in character)* How does wearing thong panties make you feel?

ALLY: Sexy.

PAULA: Do you like to feel sexy?

(ALLY reaches out for the small, plastic sprayer on a table next to her.)

ALLY: Water is sexy.

PAULA: Is it?

ALLY: *(Fondling the small spray can)* Oh yeah...steam rising up from the tub, warming your skin...the door locked... next to the toilet, I found a copy of—

PAULA: *Hustler.*

ALLY: *(Pointing the sprayer at her)* No. *Screw. Penthouse.*

PAULA: What are you doing?

ALLY: I'm going to spray you.

PAULA: Why?

ALLY: Because I want to see you wet.

PAULA: Okay, let's back-pedal a little bit here. I sense you feel threatened.

ALLY: Are you threatening me?

PAULA: Maybe you think I am. You feel you need to do something to me. You want to get me wet. So, I'll feel small…embarrassed…helpless. You want to humiliate me. *(A beat)* If it makes you feel better—

ALLY: Yes?

PAULA: Then you can spray me.

ALLY: *(Eager)* Oh, *goody*…

PAULA: But—

(ALLY's *hand freezes.*)

ALLY: What?

PAULA: Not in the face, okay?

(ALLY *pauses, frustrated. She sprays* PAULA *in the knee area.* PAULA *cries out in arousal.*)

PAULA: *(Composing herself)* So, Ally—how did that make you feel?

ALLY: Not as good as I would've liked. But that's okay. I like playing doctor with you.

PAULA: Please don't say things like that.

ALLY: Except now I think I'd like to have a *physical*…!

PAULA: As your therapist, I'm not going to be able to treat you properly if you continue to distract me.

ALLY: Yes, I understand that, but—I'm the distracting one, right? I mean I'm the nut here, right?

PAULA: Please don't refer to yourself that way.

ALLY: Do you know why I'm here?

PAULA: Yes. You claim to see visions.

ALLY: *(Amorous; checking out her legs)* Yes...yes, I see *visions...!*

PAULA: Do you want to tell me a little bit about some of these visions?

ALLY: I never remember any. They come and go. If you give me a name, I might be able to remember *something* but other than that... *(Shrugs her shoulders)*

PAULA: Yes. They overtake you in the moment. Like memory.

ALLY: Yes. They come and go.

PAULA: Yes. Like memory.

ALLY: Yes. *(A beat)* Open your legs for me.

PAULA: What did you say?

ALLY: Let me see it—

PAULA: See what?

ALLY: The monster.

PAULA: Ally—

ALLY: No? You won't show me your little monster?

PAULA: I'm not here for your amusement—don't play games.

ALLY: But you like my games.

PAULA: No one likes your games. This is serious. You've been placed here because you claim to be channeling the spirit of *Moisefina*, a converted, Sephardic nun from fifteenth century Spain.

ALLY: Holy shit.

PAULA: *(Looking through a folder)* And according to your file, before she became a nun, this *Moisefina* was some kind of a *button-weaver* and she felt the Spaniards were stealing all of her father's buttons. So, she wanted *you* to bring her as many buttons as you could. In fact, she wanted *all* the buttons in the world. And in your zeal, you tackled about three people to the ground and one of them, a local priest, sustained major nose injuries. *You almost broke his nose!*

ALLY: Well, he should've given me the fucking button then, right?

(ALLY *dissolves into laughter.* PAULA *gives her a withering look.*)

PAULA: If you can't take this seriously—

ALLY: *(Teasingly) Aww*…don't be mad…I only hurt you because I love you…

PAULA: You love me because you hurt me.

(Sound of broken glass. ALLY *has a physical reaction to this.)*

ALLY: What?

PAULA: You hurt me because you love me.

ALLY: *(Out of character)* Wait a minute…why are you saying that? That's not what you're supposed to say…

PAULA: *(Out of character as well)* What am I supposed to say?

ALLY: *(Still out of character)* What do you mean? You know…*you know*…about how I need discipline… this is the part where we talk about how I need to be *disciplined* by the hospital orderly—

PAULA: Oh. *Oh! (Back in character)* You're so undisciplined—

ALLY: Yes, yes, I am.

PAULA: You're thinking about him again, aren't you? The handsome, muscular orderly who's standing right outside this office? The one who's like He-Man?

ALLY: *(defiantly)* Maybe.

PAULA: You're thinking about him, aren't you? About what might happen if he came in here?

ALLY: Maybe I am…so what is it to you?

PAULA: You think about his wild eyes. His bulging arms and powerful chest. The hair on his legs.

ALLY: You think about him, too.

PAULA: Yes, yes you're right. I do. The one who's like He-Man?

ALLY: Yes. He-Man.

PAULA: I'm so undisciplined. Just like you. I'm a dirty girl.

ALLY: *(Echoes this)* I'm a dirty girl.

PAULA: If it was just the three of us in here, in this office…all alone…just the three of us…quiet…with the door locked—

ALLY: Maybe you should call him in.

PAULA: Now? Right now?

ALLY: Yeah. Right now. I think perhaps I *do* need discipline from the handsome, muscular hospital orderly…with the hairy legs…and the only way I'm going to get what I deserve is by having him come in and *give it to me*. Now. Where is he?

PAULA: *(Pointing towards the pitcher of juice)* He's right behind that door. He's sooo close.

ALLY: My mouth is dry.

PAULA: Are you thirsty? Thirsty for He-Man's kisses?

ALLY: Yes. Yes, I'm thirsty.

PAULA: Then have some orange juice.

(Sound of broken glass.)

ALLY: *(Suddenly frightened)* No. There was a spilled glass of orange juice on the floor.

PAULA: I bet it was really tasty.

ALLY: The orange juice was everywhere. That glass must've been filled to the top. Jagged, shiny bits scattered. All over the kitchen floor. And it frightened me. So, I just wanted to hold the loosie in my hand, you know? Not 'cause I was going to smoke it or anything. It relaxes me to just *hold it*. And then I heard—

PAULA: He-Man?

ALLY: *(Not hearing her)*…And then I heard the monster—

PAULA: *(Out of character)* No. *Goddamnit…* That's not what you're supposed to say…!

ALLY: I'm sorry…*I'm sorry*…! I forgot myself.

PAULA: *(After a pause)* It's okay…

(A long beat. The two women sit and say nothing. ALLY leans over and whispers something in PAULA's ear. PAULA smiles and nods in agreement. ALLY leans in, suggestively.)

ALLY: Monsters live in the dark.

ALLY: Yes, yes they do—you like to make me think about it, don't you?

ALLY: I do?

PAULA: Yes. You do. Don't lie. I know when you're lying. You love to lie, don't you?

ALLY: *(Excited)* When you're nervous, your bosom begins to heave…up and down.

PAULA: When you lie, your bottom lip starts to tremble and glisten… Do you like looking at my breasts?

ALLY: As much as you like looking at my lips.

PAULA: If you were a man, would you fuck me?

ALLY: I'm not a man and I'd fuck you—

PAULA: What makes you think I'd even want you?

ALLY: Nothing. Nothing at all—

PAULA: Do you think you're worthy of me?

ALLY: No. No, I don't...

PAULA: Then why did you say that?

ALLY: I'm the nut remember?

(ALLY *is trying to walk out of the room.* PAULA *blocks her.*)

PAULA: *(Aggressive with her)* Where do you think you're going, huh? We still have five minutes left.

ALLY: No, we don't.

PAULA: Yes, we do.

ALLY: We don't.

PAULA: Word association...!

ALLY: *(A death sentence) No!* Not that—anything but that!

PAULA: If I say a word to you...

ALLY: No. Don't say a word. Don't. Please don't—

PAULA: You answer me back with the first word that comes to your mind.

ALLY: No. I won't.

PAULA: Oh, yes—you will. And you'll like it.

ALLY: *(Becoming aroused)* No, I won't. Please. Don't make me.

PAULA: Stop begging. It's so pathetic.

ALLY: Please. You're so powerful. You feel you need to do something to me. So, I'll feel small...embarrassed... helpless. You want to humiliate me.

PAULA: If I say the word 'love' to you—

ALLY: I don't know—

PAULA: Oops. That's not good enough.

ALLY: You crazy bitch—

PAULA: *(Sing-song)* I need more—I want more…*give me more…!* What do you think of when I say, 'love?'

ALLY: Candlelight.

PAULA: Hot

ALLY: Burning.

PAULA: Pain.

ALLY: Sharp.

PAULA: Pointed.

ALLY: Razor.

PAULA: Broken.

ALLY: Glass.

PAULA: Wine.

ALLY: Beer.

(The sound of broken glass. This halts ALLY.)

ALLY: Beer…beer…a broken beer bottle in my face, my blood…my blood coming down my cheeks, drops of iron on my tongue. There's a piece of glass embedded in my chin—

PAULA: Wait a minute. That's not love. That's romance.

ALLY: *(Out of character)* I don't want to do this anymore! I won't do this—

PAULA: *(Out of character)* Ally, what's wrong?

ALLY: This. *This.* Isn't the orderly supposed to come in now?

PAULA: *(Out of character)* But you can't rush it. *(Low voice)* Remember, we have to do our best to keep to the session.

ALLY: *(Out of character)* I'm more than willing to keep to it. It's your dumb ass that keeps screwing it up all the time.

PAULA: Ally—I don't know how to tell you this...but the handsome and muscular hospital orderly with the hairy legs...?

ALLY: Yes, the one like He-Man?

PAULA: Yes, that one. His name is Vincent.

ALLY: Yes, I know... *(Exulting in it)* Vincent...!

PAULA: Yes. Vincent. Ally—I don't know how to tell you this...

ALLY: *(Impatient with her)* Will you just *say it*?

PAULA: Vincent is dead.

ALLY: All right then, he...He's—wait a minute. He's *what*? He's dead? *(Looking out over the audience; out of character)* Oh, so now, you're *dead*?

(Lights up on VINCENT. *Both* ALLY *and* PAULA *can see him.)*

VINCENT: *(Not looking at her; whisper)* Ssssh. I'm not here...

ALLY: Vincent—

VINCENT: *(Whisper)* Make like I'm not here *nena*, all right?

ALLY: Vincent, I'm looking right at you! Game over—

VINCENT: Come on—keep your voice down, okay?

ALLY: I'm not going to continue doing this...

VINCENT: I did the last session the way you wanted me to, right?

ALLY: Yeah, but you also said you'd be a part of it, didn't you?

VINCENT: What difference does it make?

ALLY: It makes a difference to me! You've got me playing some psycho lesbian when *she's* the one who's the nutcase!

PAULA: Okay, let's back pedal a bit here…

ALLY: *Mira nena*—I'd like to backpedal your face in, all right…?

PAULA: Ally, do I have to call in the orderly?

ALLY: There is no orderly, *estupida*! *He's* the orderly.

VINCENT: Ally, leave her alone. At least she was keeping to the session.

PAULA: What did I say at the start of our session, Ally? I can't help you if you won't help yourself…!

ALLY: *(To* VINCENT*)* Can you believe this? She's still in it! *(To* PAULA*; clapping her hands)* Mija—get a clue, we've been interrupted. The session is *over*!

VINCENT: You need to calm down, *mami*.

ALLY: Over. Over. Over. Over. Over. *Over…!*

PAULA: *(Overlapping) Okay*… There's no reason to get so upset. *(To* VINCENT*)* There's just no talking to her. She's always like this.

VINCENT: *(To* ALLY*)* I'm sorry. I should've told you I was going to be dead this time around.

PAULA: I don't see why. We almost got through the whole thing this time—

VINCENT: Well, not exactly…

PAULA: If she hadn't stopped, we would've finished.

ALLY: *(To her)* You're an idiot if you think we'll ever finish a session.

VINCENT: Okay, that's enough.

PAULA: *(Angrily)* Don't you call me an idiot! You're the idiot for stopping. We were almost finished!

ALLY: We will *never* finish a session.

VINCENT: Ally—

ALLY: It's always stop and start. Stop and start. It's always like that. It doesn't end.

PAULA: Vincent…

ALLY: Stop and start. Stop and start. Over and over again.

PAULA: Tell her to shut her mouth!

ALLY: But it's not supposed to ever *end*.

PAULA: But we *know* how it's supposed to end. With sex. We're supposed to have sex. All three of us. That's what we were told!

ALLY: And how are we supposed to do that if Vincent is *dead* during this particular session?

VINCENT: Well, you're playing a psychic, right? You see visions, right? See, in this session you're eventually supposed to use *Moisefina* to channel my spirit and then my ghost was going to descend upon all of you. It was going to be fucking hot, yo…!

ALLY: That's ridiculous. And so *cheap*.

VINCENT: What are you talking about? This is not cheap; this is some beautiful shit here. You shouldn't have stopped it, Ally.

PAULA: That's right, Ally—you shouldn't have stopped it.

VINCENT: *(Smiling at* PAULA*)* It was getting good, yo!

PAULA: I know! I thought it was getting good, too.

VINCENT: Two women, loving up on each other, feeling each other's *cositas*; she was going to tell you that she genuinely cares about you Ally, you know? Right before you was going to go down on her. I mean, what's wrong with that?

ALLY: That's not the way these things happen.

VINCENT: Who cares? It's hot.

PAULA: *(Sexily)* I think it sounds very clever, Vincent.

VINCENT: Thanks, Paula.

ALLY: *(To* PAULA*)* Uh… sweetie, you're wasting your time—he doesn't have his penis on right now.

VINCENT: *(To* ALLY*; a beat)* What the fuck are you talking about?

ALLY: Oh, you haven't noticed?

VINCENT: Noticed what?

ALLY: You don't have a penis. I don't have a pussy. And neither does she.

VINCENT: What? *(Putting his hand to his crotch)* Are you out of your fucking…? *(He can't feel anything)* Oh shit!

PAULA: *(Feeling her crotch)* Oh my Lord, she's right.

VINCENT: Oh shit!

PAULA: *(Still feeling)* I don't feel anything down there.

VINCENT: *(Looking down his pants) OH SHIT!*

PAULA: I don't understand. How can this happen?

VINCENT: *(Wailing)* Oooooh Sssssssshiiiiiiiiiiiiiiiiitttttttttt tt!!!!!!!!!!!!!!!!!

ALLY: We're not in session right now. Once we're in session, we get them back.

*(*VINCENT *places his hand on* PAULA*'S breast. Then he runs over to* ALLY *and places his hand on her breast.)*

VINCENT: Nothing. I don't feel a thing.

ALLY: Well, you don't have anything to feel with.

*(*VINCENT *starts stuffing the front of his pants with the panties from the box.)*

VINCENT: This is going too fucking far. I never noticed this bullshit before.

ALLY: We've been in session for a long time, Vincent.

VINCENT: *(In tears)* I'm going to need to speak to somebody about this shit.

ALLY: Who are you going to talk to? It's only the three of us. It's always been just the three of us.

PAULA: *(Emphatic; angrily watering the plants in the back)* I'm not going to continue doing anything without my pussy!

ALLY: We have to get back in session. If you want to feel again, you can only feel in session.

VINCENT: *(Burying his face in his hands)* I can't do this…!

ALLY: Yes, you can, Vincent. We all can.

PAULA: *(Waving her watering-can; angry)* Not without my pussy!

ALLY: You get it back in session.

(Voice-Over: Female voice)

Warning. Thirty seconds to resume session. Or risk spiritual annihilation.

VINCENT: *(Giving it the finger)* Fuck you, all right? What did you do with my dick bitch?

ALLY: *(Jumping up; getting things in order)* Okay. Let's go.

PAULA: Oh, God—not again!

ALLY: Vincent, get up…! And take those panties out of your pants we need them.

VINCENT: *(Pulling the panties out; throwing them in the box)* So, what are we doing?

VOICEOVER: 26…25…24…

ALLY: What we've always done. We need one lesbian, a straight man, and a bi-curious straight girl.

VOICEOVER: 22…21…

PAULA: I want to be the lesbian this time.

ALLY: I'm *always* the lesbian.

PAULA: Since when? We're allowed to switch, aren't we?

VINCENT: Okay, but don't complain when you're the last one to get it up the ass, all right?

VOICEOVER: 18…17…16…

ALLY: Trust me, Paula… It's never going to get that far.

PAULA: It will. Stop saying that…!

VOICEOVER: 14…13…12…

VINCENT: *(Animated)* Nah, nah, nah, nah. Listen to me, yo. I'm going to fuck the both of you sooo good and then I'm going to watch you do each other, all right? And then I'm going to fuck yous both again.

PAULA: *(Lascivious smile)* All right! I like the sound of that.

ALLY: Well, we can only hope for the best.

PAULA: *(Formally shaking hands with* ALLY*)* Good luck.

VOICEOVER: 9…8…7…6…

ALLY: *(Shaking hands back)* Oh, that's so sweet. Thanks. All the best to you, too. *(To* VINCENT*)* Good luck.

VINCENT: *(Shaking her hand)* Hey, let's do this right, mami. *(To* PAULA*; shaking her hand)* See you at the end of my cock.

PAULA: *(Big smile)* Hey, thanks—right back at you, okay?

VOICEOVER: 3…2…1… Resume Session. Line 069. Section 4. Begin.

(Lights change. ALLY, PAULA, and VINCENT gasp out loud and immediately put their hands to their crotches. Their genitalia are back. A moment as they all smile at each other; VINCENT gives the victory sign and goes out the office, closing the door behind him.)

ALLY: I think maybe you should call in the orderly.

PAULA: Now? Right now?

ALLY: Yeah. Right now. *(She looks in the direction of the voice-over. She nods reassuringly at PAULA.) (Speaking rapidly without feeling)* I think perhaps I *do* need discipline from the handsome, muscular hospital orderly and the only way I'm going to get what I deserve is by having him come in and *give it to me.* Now. Where is he?

PAULA: You know where he is, Ally. He's waiting outside. Would you like for me to call him in? I know he'd like to see you. I know he'd like to see us both.

(ALLY pantomimes for PAULA to hurry over to the door.)

(Calling off-stage) Vincent? Would you please come in now?

(VINCENT enters. Very puffed-up, very macho. He stands on one side of where ALLY is sitting and PAULA stands on the other side.)

VINCENT: *(Not a very good actor)* Uh…thank you, Doctor…. uh…Doctor...

ALLY: Rivera.

VINCENT: Uh…Doctor Rivera…right… I was starting to get a little worried. I've been waiting out there for so long. I just want to make sure you girls are okay.

PAULA: Well, we're very grateful for your presence, Vincent. Aren't we, Ally?

ALLY: *(Sultry)* Hello Vincent.

PAULA: *(Flirty)* Did you know my father's name is Vincent?

VINCENT: Get outa here.

PAULA: No, it's true. *(Noticing how handsome he is)* My goodness what a coincidence.

VINCENT: *(Smiling)* I know. It's a really small world.

PAULA: *(Laughing)* Oh God, tell me about it. By the way, what's that cologne you're wearing? It's absolutely amazing.

VINCENT: Thanks—

PAULA: *(Still flirty)* No, really. It's starting to make me feel a little dizzy. But I mean that in a good way…!

ALLY: Paula—*you're the lesbian*…! *(To herself)* Fucking idiot.

PAULA: *(In realization)* Oh my God—I forgot!

VINCENT: *(Hastily)* It's okay… Be cool. We just got to regroup. *Regroup—*

(ALLY *and* PAULA *switch places.* VINCENT *directs all of his macho attention towards* ALLY *now. The lines are repeated rapidly.*)

PAULA: Hello Vincent.

ALLY: Did you know my father's name is Vincent?

VINCENT: Get outa here.

ALLY: No, it's true. *(Noticing how handsome he is)* My goodness—what a coincidence.

VINCENT: *(Smiling)* I know. It's a really small world.

ALLY: *(Laughing)* Oh God, tell me about it. By the way, what's that cologne you're wearing? It's absolutely amazing.

VINCENT: Thanks—

ALLY: *(Flirty)* No, really. It's starting to make me feel a little dizzy. But I mean that in a good way…!

VINCENT: My mother gave it to me for Christmas.

PAULA: Your mother? *How sweet!*

VINCENT: Yeah. My mother—so… What seems to be the problem, Doctor Rivera?

PAULA: Please sit down, Vincent. I'm afraid I have a patient who's not responding to treatment the way she should.

VINCENT: Oooh, well we can't have that, now can we?

ALLY: Nooo…!

VINCENT: Nooo… We're going to have to do something about that, aren't we?

ALLY: I want the spray…

PAULA: *(Firmly)* No. No spray.

ALLY: Spray!

PAULA: I said no! This isn't the time for that!

VINCENT: What is she talking about?

PAULA: Oh no, no, no—please don't fret, Vincent… It's all part of Ally's treatment; if she finds herself faced with a hostile, or disturbing…or *stimulating* element in this room then she has the permission to spray at whatever it is that's *arousing* her, with this… *(Shows him a common spray bottle filled with water)*

VINCENT: I see. That's interesting.

ALLY: And it could be sexy. *(Taking off her sweater)* Especially if you spray the front of my top.

PAULA: *(Jealously)* No, Ally—we're not going to do that right now.

ALLY: Well, what does Vincent want? Maybe he wants what I want—

PAULA: I DON'T CARE WHAT YOU WANT! This is my office and we do *WHAT I WANT!* And if I want to, *I will* spray the front of your shirt!

(PAULA sprays the front of ALLY's shirt. ALLY cries out in arousal. VINCENT grabs the spray bottle and sets it down.)

VINCENT: *(Caressing the both of them; laughing)* Now ladies please—I'm sure we'll be able to work this out. There's enough of me to go around for the two of you.

PAULA: *(Sighing)* I'm very fond of Ally, but she's a difficult patient. I'm so glad you're here to control the situation, Vincent.

VINCENT: *(To her)* What is Ally short for?

ALLY: Alicia…

VINCENT: Oh, that's beautiful… *(Taking a moment; looking at her)* You look tired.

ALLY: I'm all right.

PAULA: *(Flirty)* How do I look?

VINCENT: Hey, you look hot, *mami*…!

ALLY: Paula—

PAULA: I know, I know—*I'm the lesbian*…! I don't think this was such a good idea; I should've let you be the lesbian again.

ALLY: *(Shrugs)* Too late. Just go with it.

VINCENT: Ally…Alicia…*Alicia*… That's my Mom's name. My Moms is a quiet woman. A quiet, *passive* woman. She doesn't talk back, she doesn't quarrel— she's always been real smart. It's what I've always loved about her. She's been a great mother to my two little sisters, Graciela and Myrna.

PAULA: *(Little gushy)* Aw, you have sisters?

VINCENT: *(Taking out his wallet; proudly)* Yeah. My two Boricua belles; that's what I call them.

PAULA: *(Looking at the pictures)* Oh my goodness, look at these precious little angels. Just like two pretty little senoritas in a row. It looks like you have a lovely family.

VINCENT: I'd like to have a son someday. My Pops always says that you're not really a man without a son, you know? You got to have a little man who looks like you to make you proud, right? *Tienes ser un hombre bien macho, tu sabes?* And oh man, let me tell you; my Moms can *cook* like you wouldn't believe. I mean, she can make an *arroz con habichuelas* that'll make you weep, you know what I'm saying?

PAULA: Of course. We both understand don't we Ally?

ALLY: Am I the only one who's noticed that it's not so sexy in here anymore?

VINCENT: Aw man—that's my bad. I'm really sorry. I just...I didn't know your name was Alicia, all right? Alicia... That's my mother's name... She's... I can't fuck you and be seeing my mother at the same time, you know?

PAULA: What? Are you kidding me?

ALLY: What are you talking about? You've known what my name was all along.

VINCENT: No, man—I knew your name was Ally, but I didn't know it was a nickname—

ALLY: You *gave* me the nickname!

VINCENT: I didn't know, all right? I can't just do this—I can't just fuck you and then go home and look my Moms in the face. It's not right. I'm a good man. I can't do this shit.

ALLY: Wait a minute. You think you're going somewhere? *(Laughs)* Hold it. Where exactly do you think you're going?

VINCENT: I have a home. Okay? I have a place to go. Everybody's got *someplace* to go.

PAULA: We don't.

VINCENT: That's bullshit. If you want to believe that crap, go ahead. But I don't have any more time to waste here with you two. I got people at home waiting for me.

ALLY: No, Vincent. They're not.

VINCENT: Don't make me have to smack you, all right? Look at these pictures—

ALLY: We have.

PAULA: And we love them.

ALLY: Just like we love you.

VINCENT: They exist, okay? They're here. They're alive. They're my whole life.

VOICEOVER: Warning. Thirty seconds to resume session. Or risk spiritual annihilation.

PAULA: Damn it. We have to start another one. Jesus— why can't we ever *finish* one of these?

VOICEOVER: Warning. Thirty seconds to resume session. Or risk spiritual annihilation.

VINCENT: *(Yelling out; to voice-over) And you need to shut the fuck up, all right?* It's not going to work anymore. I'm not resuming shit. You don't scare me; none of this bullshit scares me.

ALLY: Vincent—

VINCENT: I have people waiting for me. I know who I am.

ALLY: Vincent, just think about this for a second…I don't think we're here. I don't think we *even exist*…!

(A beat. PAULA *nervously returns to spraying and watering her plants, while watching the two of them.* VINCENT *stares at* ALLY. *)*

VINCENT: You are one sick bitch you know that?

PAULA: *(To the plants; nervous baby-talk)* Who's my little *sweetie yum-yum*, hmm? Who needs some *wah-wah*?

ALLY: I'm not trying to hurt you, Vincent.

VINCENT: Bullshit—

ALLY: I'm trying to be as honest with you as I possibly—

VINCENT: *(Cutting her off; laughs)* Honest? You two bitches?

ALLY: Vincent, listen to me—

VINCENT: I grew up with bitches like you.

ALLY: Did you?

VINCENT: Oh, yeah. Women are liars. They say they want you to be the man, to take care of them, to show them respect. But as soon as you turn your back—

ALLY: Who are you talking about?

VINCENT: You bitches are always there…messing things up for everybody. Always showing your *cositas*—

ALLY: Paula and I have always been *here*. *With you*!

PAULA: *(Quietly)* You have to stop this. You'll bring back the monster.

VINCENT: Stop talking that shit. There is no monster.

PAULA: *(In shock)* Don't you hear him?

VINCENT: No!

PAULA: Oh my God. You're so lucky…
He screams out from my chest. He's always there.

ALLY: He reaches his arm across my torso…
And squeezes my left nipple between his fingers…

PAULA: And when I yell out in pain—

ALLY: He doesn't know whether to cry or laugh…
Because his feelings are so mixed up…

PAULA: But he's *still* the monster.

ALLY: And I can feel his hard, sharp knee…
Propped up against the small of my back…
As he hisses in my ear, "No one will ever love you like
I do, you know. You can never be free…"

VINCENT: Stop it—

PAULA: His breath chills the back of my neck. Like hot
ice. "You can never be free…"

VINCENT: I said, stop! Please—

ALLY: *(Grabbing the box of panties; pulling one out)* I don't
think there's a home for you. Not anymore.

VINCENT: *(In anguish)* Don't fucking say that, all right?

ALLY: You just wouldn't be here if you still *belonged*.

VINCENT: So, what the fuck are you saying? We're in
hell?

PAULA: *(To him)* Well, it's not heaven, is it my little
sweetie-sweets? Nooooo, it's not…! *(A beat)* It's going to
be okay, *Papi*. Have some orange juice.

VINCENT: Stop that. I don't want any orange juice. I
hate orange juice.

ALLY: *(Pulling out a pair of panties; holding it out to
VINCENT)* Look, it's going to be okay. I'm pretty sure I
wore this one all ready, so just sniff the crotch and let's
get going here.

VINCENT: Get that away from me.

ALLY: We're going to get through one of these if it kills me. Now, *smell it*…!

VINCENT: And don't tell me what to do.

ALLY: Why not?

VINCENT: You're a woman. A woman doesn't tell a man what to do.

ALLY: You don't like having a woman suddenly take control? You don't think that's sexy? A lot of men think that's sexy—

VINCENT: Yeah, maybe so, but—

ALLY: Don't you think a woman should be able to stand up for herself if she needs to? Don't you think that's important?

VINCENT: *(She's confusing him)* I don't know. I don't know what you're talking about. Come on—

ALLY: Don't you think you're going to have to make a choice? Don't you think you'll have to make up your mind? Which is the ideal woman for you—*passive or strong*? *(A beat; in an ominous tone)* Or is it that she just has to be *straight*?

VINCENT: Shut your fucking mouth, all right?

PAULA: Stop it—Stop this!

ALLY: No, because I really want to know, Vincent… Just what the hell is it that you want?

PAULA: *(Getting between them)* He wants a threesome…!

ALLY: Paula, for God's sakes…!

PAULA: You're not the only one who needs to get laid, you know? On second thought, I don't want to be the lesbian… I want to be the confused, straight girl.

ALLY: Well, that's good 'cause that's exactly what you are, Paula—*you fucking idiot*…!

PAULA: You're just jealous because I'm cuter than you are.

ALLY: *(Sarcastic)* Oh yeah, that must be it.

VINCENT: What the fuck is this? Now you're going after each other?

PAULA: *(To* VINCENT*)* I'm upset, okay? *I need to vent…!*

VINCENT: I don't even want to have sex with the two of you.

ALLY: Exactly. I feel the same way about you.

PAULA: So do I. Fuck you both.

VOICEOVER: *(Female voice)* Repeat. Warning. Thirty seconds to resume session. Or risk spiritual annihilation.

PAULA: *(To* ALLY*)* You see? We're in trouble again, thanks to you.

ALLY: *(To* PAULA*)* I'm really beginning to hate you… you know that?

VOICEOVER: 26…25…24…

PAULA: I don't care.

ALLY: We're all responsible for finishing a session, you know. I'm not the only one here.

VINCENT: *(Feeling his crotch)* Wait a minute… wait a minute—

PAULA: I'm not going to let you bring the monster back.

ALLY: That's not what I'm trying to do. *I want to finish the session!*

VOICEOVER: 24…23…22…

PAULA: No, you don't. If you did, you wouldn't keep ruining it for everyone.

ALLY: I hate you.

PAULA: I hate you, too.

VINCENT: *(With his hand at his crotch; rubbing)* I can still feel it. It's still there. Oh my God. *I can feel it.* It's warm and pulsating. Hairy. It throbs... And...and...Oooh! Ooooh!

PAULA: We're going to end up getting into trouble because you can't follow the rules.

VOICEOVER: 18...17...16...

VINCENT: *(His hand down his pants; still rubbing)* Ooooh! Ooooh—yeah!

ALLY: Vincent, could you keep it down, please? We're trying to talk.

PAULA: I have nothing more to say to you.

ALLY: Fine.

VOICEOVER: 13...12...11...

VINCENT: *(He's finished)* Ooooh, man—*yeah!*

ALLY: *(Realizing)* Wait a minute. Vincent, *what are you doing?*

PAULA: Oh, no...!

VOICEOVER: 8...7...6...

VINCENT: *(Closing his pants)* Oh man—what a relief, yo!

ALLY: You're masturbating!

PAULA: Oh my God...!

VOICEOVER: 2...1...

(Lights change. There is a spot on a puzzled VINCENT. He looks over the audience.)

VINCENT: But it was there. It was there. And I could feel it. What the fuck else was I supposed to do with it?

VOICEOVER: Spiritual annihilation now commencing.

(Blackout. Supernatural music. Lights back up. VINCENT *is nowhere to be seen. Both* ALLY *and* PAULA *are in the same spots they were in before the lights went out. A beat.)*

PAULA: *(Weakly)* Vincent? Where are you? Where is he?

ALLY: He's gone.

PAULA: *(Running around the room)* Oh my God…
Vincent? VINCENT! *(Angrily; to* ALLY*)* THIS IS ALL
YOUR FAULT!

ALLY: Calm down.

PAULA: *(Hysterical)* That's it. The monster's coming.
We're done for.

ALLY: Do you know what the monster is, Paula?

PAULA: *(Covering her ears)* No. Don't say a word.

ALLY: The monster is a little like love.
But it's a love you think you can do without.
Until you have it.
Monsters live in the dark.
…And in the dark, they breathe holes into the walls.
And then all the white plaster inside your wall turns to
powder.
And the monster's breath becomes a stinging wasp.
And that wasp can build a nest deep inside your wall.
And they all stay there…together…like a family…all
of them tunneling into the alabaster, the grains raining
over their prickly wings like dirty, grubby snow.
And as you listen—with the side of your head up
against the partition; listening to that awful buzzing…
It turns into a kind of music you never needed to hear,
with its little tune being drummed into the sides of
your stomach.
And *that's* the monster.
That's the monster, okay?

(A beat)

VOICEOVER: Warning. Twenty seconds to resume session. Or risk spiritual annihilation.

PAULA: Twenty? But they always gave us at least thirty—

ALLY: *(Sad smile)* We've been bad—

VOICEOVER: 17…16…15…

PAULA: *(Frantic)* But we don't have a third person!

ALLY: We do. They wouldn't start otherwise…

VOICEOVER: 13…12…11…

PAULA: Well, then where is he? I don't see anybody!

ALLY: I know you're scared. But you have to calm down.

VOICEOVER: 9…8…7…

PAULA: I'm frightened.

ALLY: I know. So am I.

PAULA: I don't know what to do.

VOICEOVER: 4…3…2…1…

ALLY: You'll be all right. Just be horny.

VOICEOVER: Resume Session. Line 070. Section 5. Begin.

(A beat. Lights change. At the same time, both PAULA *and* ALLY *gasp out loud and place their hands on their crotches. However, they sit frozen on stage; they don't know what to do.)*

VOICEOVER: Resume Session. Line 070. Section 5. Begin.

PAULA: *(Weakly)* What am I supposed to say?

(A beat. It looks like PAULA *and* ALLY *will remain frozen in their places.)*

PAULA: *(Near tears)* What do I say?

(A beat)

ALLY: *(Sad and resigned)* How I need discipline...how I need to be *disciplined* by the hospital orderly—

PAULA: *(Mechanical)* The handsome, muscular orderly who's standing right outside this office? The one who's like He-Man?

ALLY: *(The same)* Yes. He-Man.

PAULA: You think about his wild eyes. His bulging arms and powerful chest. The hair on his legs.

ALLY: You think about him, too.

PAULA: Do you feel close to He-Man?

ALLY: Yes, I feel close to him... *(A beat. She turns to look at* PAULA.*)* Are we close?

PAULA: I've already told you not to flirt with me.

ALLY: You like it.

PAULA: Yes. I like it very much. But we really have to continue our session.

ALLY: Do we?

PAULA: Should I call in the muscular, hospital orderly...with the hairy legs?

ALLY: Maybe you should.

PAULA: Now? Right now?

ALLY: Yeah. Right now. I think perhaps I *do* need discipline from the handsome, muscular hospital orderly...with the hairy legs...and the only way I'm going to get what I deserve is by having him come in and *give it to me.* Now. Where is he?

PAULA: He's right behind that door.

(A beat. PAULA *leans over and kisses* ALLY. *It is a long, lingering and romantic kiss. At that moment, we hear loud, horrible groans and moans coming from the other side of the office door. The doorknob rattles violently and the pounding*

upon the door borders on the brutal. It is the monster. But the two women appear to be oblivious to all this as they continue to kiss and caress one another.)

(Lights change. A soft glow descends upon the stage. Almost as if in a dream. ALLY *and* PAULA *begin to move in a slower, sensual motion. Touching each other's faces and hair, shoulders, neck, etc.* VINCENT *appears. He stares intently at the two women. He addresses the audience.)*

VINCENT: And then I heard the monster…
The sounds of moans coming from the bedroom…
It sounded like a woman.
My Dad was in the bedroom with another bitch, you know?
That had to be it.
And then my Moms would come home and he would beat on her.
Again… *I fucking hated him so much—*
I picked it up from the floor.
I didn't care about the orange juice. I picked it up.
The biggest, shiniest piece of glass. The largest slice.
Because I was going to go into that bedroom and kill him—

ALLY: Oh poor Vincent—

PAULA: You were only fourteen years old…

ALLY: What did you know about killing anybody?

VINCENT: *(Suddenly childlike)* No, man—check this out—it was going to be great.
Just like *Oedipus Rex!*
I was going to kill the father in order to protect the mother.
I was going to be a *real man*.
For my Moms, you know?
He was never going to be able to beat up on us ever again, yo…!

PAULA: *(Hopeful)* Never again?

VINCENT: Never, *never* again…!

PAULA: Sweet, little Vincent—

ALLY: *(Smile)* Maybe you should've just cleaned up the orange juice…

VINCENT: I opened the door.
All I could hear was my heart beating
And something like close to the ocean in my ears.

ALLY: *(Voice-Over)* My sweet Vincent—

VINCENT: But it wasn't my Dad.
It was you two.
I saw you two—
My Moms and her friend Titi Paola…
They were naked.
They were kissing.
And…they looked *damn good.*

(ALLY *and* PAULA *laugh softly and continue embracing each other.*)

VINCENT: I couldn't keep standing there staring.
No matter how much I wanted to.
I ran to the bathroom.
I had so many questions stuck in my throat.
But whom the hell was I going to ask?
Did my Moms know she was a dyke?
Did my Dad know?
Is that why he fucked around so much?
If gay guys have *beards*, then was my Dad like my Mom's *wig*?

(ALLY *and* PAULA *laugh again and begin to touch and caress* VINCENT. *Not sexually, but in a more good-natured and familial manner.*)

VINCENT: Was this my Mom's way of getting even with my Dad? Or was she in love with Titi Paola? Paola was

so *beautiful*... She had long, dark hair. Bedroom hair.
Sex hair, you know? And my Moms, with her jet-black
eyes and nut-brown skin...

(ALLY *and* PAULA *move away from* VINCENT. ALLY *goes
back to her chair and book.* PAULA *returns to watering her
plants. As in the start of the play.* VINCENT *stands center
stage and continues to speak to the audience. Playwright's
note: At this point, the women's lines will be as recorded
voice-overs only with the actors mimicking their earlier
movements from the start of the play. They may be mouthing
their lines as well.)*

VINCENT: I sat on the floor of the bathroom.
I slipped my hand in my pants.
And I could feel it. *I felt it.*
I started to touch myself.

Thinking about Paola's hair and my Mom's skin.
I kept touching myself.
I couldn't help it.
When it was all over, I sat there on that bathroom floor
and I cried.
'Cause maybe my Dad was right, you know?
Maybe I did want to do to my Mom what the guy
In *Oedipus Rex*, does to his Mom, you know?
And that's *sick*, right?
That's when I took the piece of glass out of my
pocket—

VOICEOVER: (PAULA) We can't keep interrupting the
session.

VOICEOVER: (ALLY) This is so much easier to do without
memory. But memory is all Vincent has—

VINCENT: I stabbed it.
My *thing*.
I stabbed it, you know?
The first time I brought the point of it down hard.
Real hard.

But the second and third time, it was like I couldn't feel anything.

There was something sticky and wet on my fingers.

I couldn't look down. My body went cold.

Then the monster came and took me.

His breath gave me chills me on the back of my neck.

Like hot ice. "You can never be free…"

VOICEOVER: (PAULA. *To the plants*) My darlings would never want to be free of me…Right, my *sweeties*? *My precious little kumquats…!*

VINCENT: I couldn't look down. I was such a coward. My own blood frightened me. And I don't mean the family blood that tied us all together. Just the blood that was supposed to be fucking mine to keep…!

VOICEOVER: (PAULA. *Clipping dead leaves off a plant; to herself*) It's important to know how to adapt. What do you do if you're trapped amongst a pack of wolves?

VOICEOVER: (ALLY) You howl your ass off.

VINCENT: And when I opened my eyes again, I was *here*—

VOICEOVER: (ALLY) It's just like real life.

VINCENT: I was here.

With you two.

With Ally and Paula. It's *always* been the three of us.

VOICEOVER: Warning. Thirty seconds to resume session. Or risk spiritual annihilation.

VOICEOVER: (PAULA) We have to do our best to keep to the next session.

VOICEOVER: (ALLY) I'm more than willing to keep to it. It's your dumb ass that keeps screwing it up all the time.

VOICEOVER: (PAULA) Why do you talk to me like that? Vincent, tell Ally not to speak to me like that—

VOICEOVER: 27...26...25...

VINCENT: (To audience) I love hearing women talk shit.

VOICEOVER: (ALLY) The last time I was this frightened I was little. Okay, maybe not so little. Maybe I was thirt-five. Actually, I don't remember how old I was. But my husband was drunk on beer. And he could be *vicious* when he was drunk. He insisted that I sit across from him this one time. I don't remember what we talked about. It didn't matter—

VINCENT: (Sitting across from her; sad smile) Memories don't matter, *Alicia*. Not here—

VOICEOVER: 19...18...17...

VOICEOVER: (ALLY) But at one point, he held the beer bottle up...and I knew. I *knew* that any second now it was going to be smashed in my face. All I could do was wait for it. And the whole time, I kept thinking, "What did I do? What horrible things did I do to make you want to smash a beer bottle right into my face, *Papi*?"

VINCENT: (Softly; sad smile) I would never hurt you, *Mami*... (As though singing a song; softly) Tu eres una Santa; mi estrella, un poder divino—

VOICEOVER: 11...10...9...

VOICEOVER: (ALLY) Como una pendeja!

VOICEOVER: (PAULA) (Her attention still on the plants) My little blossom bundt cake... How I love you so! With your jet-black eyes and nut-brown skin—

VOICEOVER: 4...3...2...1... Resume Session. Line 070. Section 5. Begin.

(A beat. Lights change. ALLY, VINCENT and PAULA gasp out loud and place their hands on their crotches. However, they all remain frozen on stage.)

VOICEOVER: Resume Session. Line 070. Section 5. Begin.

(VINCENT *reaches over and begins to caress* ALLY *in a sexual manner. She reaches out for him as well.* PAULA *remains frozen in her place among the plants.*)

VINCENT: Ssssh, don't move.

VOICEOVER: (ALLY) But… The monster—

VOICEOVER: (PAULA) Please… I don't want the monster to come back…

(VINCENT *continues touching* ALLY. *He slips his hand into his pants and begins to caress himself.*)

VINCENT: Ssssh let him come. Its okay, *Mami.* Let him come…

VOICEOVER: (PAULA. *Speaking to her plants*) What does that mean? Spiritual annihilation?

VOICEOVER: (ALLY) Does it frighten you?

VOICEOVER: (PAULA) (*Nodding, still not looking at her*) If I knew what it was, I bet I'd be terrified.

VOICEOVER: (ALLY. *Smile*) I used to think the exact same thing about sex.

VINCENT: (*Still caressing himself*) Ssssh, its okay. Nothing will happen, *Mami.* It's okay…I can…I can…I can feel it, *Mami*… I can feel it. I feel it. (*In a quietly triumphant tone*) *I feel it.*

(*Lights down. The stage is left in blackout.*)

END OF PLAY

LAZARUS
DISPOSED

LAZARUS DISPOSED was first produced as part of the 14th International Women's Playwriting Festival (Producing Artistic Director, Vanessa Gilbert) at Perishable Theatre in Providence, Rhode Island on 2 October 2008. The cast and creative contributors were:

Bethany ....D'Arcy Dersham
Ferdinand .... Patrick Harrison
The Man... Luis A. Astudillo

Director..Beth F Milles
Stage manager ....Amanda Weir
Costume designer ....Amy Lynn Budd
Scenic design... Maggie Pilat
Lighting designer ....John Boomer
Sound designer...Terrence Shea.

CHARACTERS & SETTING

BETHANY, *late 20s-early 30s. The Unfaithful Wife.
Beautiful, dark, guilt-ridden and intense.*

FERDINAND, *late 20s-early 30s. The Best Friend. Verbose
and insecure; plus, he thinks he's funny.*

THE MAN, *late 20s, early 30s straight-thru to 40s. A
Mysterious Visitor. He's come to be of help…maybe.*

*Time and place: The action takes place in a kitchen that's in
full disarray.*

The ultimate aim of all love affairs...is more important than all other aims in man's life; and therefore it is quite worthy of the profound seriousness with which everyone pursues it.
Arthur Schopenauer

(An odd, teeny sound is heard. It's a cross between a whistle, a breath, and a sob. Lights up. A kitchen in full disarray. There are men's clothes everywhere, socks, pants, shoes and shirts almost completely cover the room. There's even a clothesline hung across the room with socks, shirts, and vests hanging upon it. A man and a woman stand in the middle of the room, they are leaning over the kitchen sink, listening. They are both dressed in elaborate black mourning.)

BETHANY: It's been making that noise for days now—

FERDINAND: I don't hear it any longer.

BETHANY: I think something's stuck in the garbage disposal.

FERDINAND: Like what?

BETHANY: I don't know.

FERDINAND: Your wedding ring?

BETHANY: *(This pains her)* Don't say that.

FERDINAND: I noticed you're not wearing it.

BETHANY: I feel ashamed.

FERDINAND: Have you called the plumber?

BETHANY: I can't find the number. I've never had to do that before…it was always Jack who took care of all the repairs in the house.

FERDINAND: Jack—

(FERDINAND bursts into tears at the name. BETHANY immediately embraces him and begins to whisper soft, smooth words of comfort to the man; crying in her arms.)

BETHANY: *(Soothingly)* It's alright.

FERDINAND: I promised myself I wouldn't do this.

BETHANY: I understand.

FERDINAND: Oh my God—

BETHANY: Just get it all out; you'll feel better…

FERDINAND: Feel better? Look at me! Look at my face—
I'm like quivering jellyfish.

BETHANY: You're upset.

FERDINAND: Well, I have good reason.

BETHANY: You're not the only one. I lost my husband.
*(She begins to fold sweaters in a methodical, almost
mechanical manner.)*

FERDINAND: I lost my best friend. My face—

BETHANY: Your face is FINE.
I'm the one who needs to fix my face.
I need to use the bathroom.

FERDINAND: Go ahead—

(We see that his casual response irritates BETHANY *on an
almost physical level. She rapidly unfolds all the sweaters
and begins refolding them again. A beat.)*

BETHANY: I can't. I can't get in; it's locked and I can't
get in.

FERDINAND: *(A beat; he begins to join her in folding clothes)*
Did you knock?

BETHANY: Of course. And I hear movement inside—

FERDINAND: Obviously there must be someone in
there…

BETHANY: *(With sudden violence)* WELL, OF COURSE
THERE'S SOMEONE IN THERE! *(To him; still and
severe)* There's someone in the bathroom and because
of that, I can't get in.

(A beat. FERDINAND *regards* BETHANY *with admiration and longing.)*

FERDINAND: You're so intense.

BETHANY: *(She returns to folding clothes; serene once more)* I know. Jack always hated that about me.

FERDINAND: No, I think it's wonderful. You're such a spark plug.

BETHANY: I've paid for my sparks.

FERDINAND: I love you.

BETHANY: Please don't say that to me. We have to decide what to do with his clothes.

FERDINAND: *(Pulling a shirt out of her hands)* But I haven't said it all day—

BETHANY: *(Taking it back)* So many clothes…I never realized he had so many—what will I do with all of them? It's too much…!

FERDINAND: But Bethany—

BETHANY: No. Not now. Save it for later. After everyone's gone.

FERDINAND: The wake ended hours ago. Everyone's already left.

BETHANY: Except for the one in the bathroom. I know it's a man. I yelled out, "Excuse me is there somebody in there?" And if it had been a woman, I would have heard her voice… She probably would've said something like, "I'll be right out," or "Just a minute." In other words, she would've been *polite*…! But all I can hear is *breathing*…heavy, masculine breathing and something like a grunt, some kind of a grunt, a few fierce little mumbles…and…and then, when I rattle the knob a little bit I see that the door has been locked and then I hear another grunt! And *that's* when I knew there must be some ill-mannered man in my bathroom and he's locked himself in. And he refuses to answer my question. A simple question! God…that upset me so much that I screamed…you didn't hear me screaming?

FERDINAND: Okay. Calm down.

BETHANY: *(Yelling; towards bathroom)* There are other people out here *WAITING,* you know! *(Back to* FERDINAND; *whisper)* I didn't see the person inside. I never even *saw* anyone go in. But he's in there. I'm sure of it.

FERDINAND: I've already counted about ten pairs of socks, six dress shirts, and four suit jackets, but I can only find these two pairs of pants. Your husband only had two pairs of pants? In his whole life? How is that possible? Is this all there is?

BETHANY: *(Towards the bathroom; still to herself)* My God, what arrogance…! Doesn't he realize how upsetting this has all been? Doesn't he know how difficult it is to plan and arrange a wake? All the expenses; the phone calls, a new black dress, nylons, flowers, a priest, a bottle of wine, not to mention, all those little white plastic cups…! But I had no choice. My husband's disappeared. He's gone.

FERDINAND: Perhaps funerals make the person in the bathroom queasy.

BETHANY: *(To him)* This wasn't a funeral. It was a memorial service.

FERDINAND: Same thing—

BETHANY: *(Offended)* No, it's NOT. Don't say that. It's not the same thing at all. Not at all. With a funeral, there's a body present. There's always a BODY. Do you see a body here? No. Are we driving to the cemetery now to put a body into the ground? No. We're not doing that, because the body is not *present*…

it's missing…it's gone astray…it's lost…disposed.
This was a memorial service. And with a memorial
service, there's no body. There's nothing. There's only
remembrance…memories…marks of respect…

(A small silence between BETHANY *and* FERDINAND.*)*

BETHANY: He found your letter, you know.

FERDINAND: My letter?

BETHANY: Yes. Your letter.

FERDINAND: What letter?

BETHANY: The letter where you said I was your *booty
charm*…

FERDINAND: *(Puzzled)* My booty charm?

BETHANY: Your *tasty fun good rice candy*…?

FERDINAND: *(Remembering)* Oooooh—

BETHANY: Your *magical mojo mistress*… Well? Do you
remember now? Are you laughing? What's so funny?
You think this is funny? It's not funny! This is probably
all your fault.

FERDINAND: You accepted my letters quickly enough.

BETHANY: I was feeling vulnerable.

FERDINAND: You're as vulnerable as a dragon.

BETHANY: That's a cruel statement.

FERDINAND: How was I to know you'd leave my letters
lying around where Jack could find them?

BETHANY: I don't leave things lying around!

FERDINAND: Don't do this now. Please.

BETHANY: You're the reason he's gone—

FERDINAND: You're not the only one who's hurting.

BETHANY: Jack hated your constantly hanging around.
Always making eyes at me—right in front of him

sometimes! Always insisting on staying over for dinner. Always trying to distract him with your silly jokes, "How many surrealists does it take to screw on a light bulb?" How stupid!

FERDINAND: You never understood the punch line—

BETHANY: What is the punch line?

FERDINAND: FISHSTICKS!

BETHANY: That's stupid!

FERDINAND: That's *surreal*! Jack got it—he loved my jokes. He always laughed!

BETHANY: To your face. He'd laugh in front of you and then as soon as you'd leave—he'd mock you...!

FERDINAND: I'm warning you. .

BETHANY: He called you a loser. Ferdinand the Loser.

FERDINAND: I won't be your flunky.

BETHANY: He couldn't stand the sight of you anymore...!

FERDINAND: Shut up—

BETHANY: You were a disgrace as his best friend!

FERDINAND: *(Brutal outburst)* And you can't plan for shit! As far as wakes go, THIS WAS CRAP. Look at this place! You're a terrible hostess. You look like a whore. You reek of alcohol and old peanuts. Why didn't you serve hors'doeurves? Something in between all the tears and lamentation...white flowers instead of red ones, you dumb slut...maybe even a few soothing hymns playing in the background.

BETHANY: *(Angrily)* Don't talk to me like that...!

FERDINAND: That's what wives are supposed to do at these things!

BETHANY: I KNOW WHAT WIVES DO!

FERDINAND: Do you? You could've cleaned the place up...you could've spoken to people rather than beating your chest and shrieking at everybody like some crazy banshee...!

BETHANY: Put my husband's pants down.

FERDINAND: Why should I?

BETHANY: You're not fit to touch his things!

FERDINAND: You can't be trusted to take care of his laundry. Your mother-in-law had to sit on a hill of socks and tightie-whities...your uncle was forced to place his hat on top of sweatshirts and fuzzy neckties...!

BETHANY: Give me those pants.

FERDINAND: No.

BETHANY: GIVE ME THE DAMN PANTS!

FERDINAND: (*dangling them in front of her; mocking*) Come and get them.

(*A fight ensues. Eventually* BETHANY *and* FERDINAND *end up on the floor, struggling with the pair of pants between them. Soon, their thrashing begins to turn into something else. They gradually become aware of the scent coming off of the pants and this begins to change the physical dynamic of their scrap. He rubs his face against the material, and then takes a long, deep, noisy and almost raucous inhale. She slips her head inside the pants. He follows suit. We can no longer see their heads since they're now both inside the pants. There is something both erotic and vulgar in the way they embrace each other even though their heads can no longer be seen. Her head pops out of the pants, and she finally manages to tug them away from him. We can see that they are both profoundly moved.*)

BETHANY: (*Deep inhale*) I miss him. I miss him so much.

FERDINAND: I miss him, too. Give me that. *(Grabs hold of a pant leg and inhales deeply; short beat)* Oh God…it smells so good.

BETHANY: *(Still smelling)* I know. It's good. It's so good.

FERDINAND: I miss him so much!

BETHANY: It smells so good. *(Inhale)*

FERDINAND: Sacred chlorine… *(Another deep inhale)*… immaculate fleece…like you laundered them at the bottom of a holy, sanctified ocean…

(BETHANY slowly rises from the floor and moves towards the kitchen sink; she holds her husband's pants close to her chest, almost reverentially.)

(The following is a series of slightly overlapping monologues between BETHANY and FERDINAND. When the overlapping starts is featured in the directions within the passages.)

BETHANY:
I always washed his clothes special right here
Right over the sink.
He would stand by and gaze at me
As I'd watch all the dirt submerge

(FERDINAND begins his passage at this point)

BETHANY: Right down all the way through the drain. With the garbage disposal tightly shut off.

FERDINAND:
We'd go to all those open-Mic nights together
Down at the Comedy Club
And we'd sit there and laugh into our beers until after midnight
He knew their Happy Hour chicken wings and multiple sauces were my favorite

(BETHANY continues at this point.)

FERDINAND: That's why he always called me "Wing Man." *(Laughs)*

BETHANY: He called me, "The Super Sluicer" *(Laughs)*
he said I could sluice his clothes better than any
Chinese laundry ever could.
Better than Woolite.
It's because I take each item of clothing and I roll it into
a stiff cylinder.
And then I begin to gently squeeze.
I squeeze right from the head of the roll, all the way
down to its length.

(FERDINAND comes in.)

BETHANY: I *squeeze* my fingers down and down and
push the water out with all the care of my limited
upbringing.

FERDINAND: His favorite sauce was the Super-Spicy
Southwestern chipotle
And mine was the 3-Alarm Tabasco.
Both of them so easily burned the insides of our
mouths.
We'd each take shots of our favorite sauce
And see how long the other could go without taking a
drink.
I always lost.

(BETHANY continues from here)

FERDINAND: I always lost.
Eventually, I'd have to press the chilled beer glass up
against my tongue...! *(Stifles a sob)*

BETHANY: I press and press and *press* against the
wringing fabric
Gently stroking away all the succulence.
Until all my gripping and clutching finally releases the
cloth ions back into the air, stripped down to its naked,
exposed threads...sparkling, hygienic, and completely
sanitized.
He loved the way I did this.

(A short beat)

FERDINAND: *(Longingly)* Yes. I always loved watching you sluice your husband's load—

BETHANY: And now it's over.

FERDINAND: It's us now. Just the two of us.

BETHANY: And what about the person in the bathroom?

FERDINAND: Oh—FORGET THE BATHROOM!

(The odd, teeny sound is suddenly heard again. Again, it's a cross between a whistle, a breath, and a sob. Both BETHANY *and* FERDINAND *hear this and are startled out of their clinch. Curious, they look at each other and then slowly turn towards the kitchen sink. They hear the sound again. A beat. They both slowly move towards the sink and gradually bend their heads down towards the sink as though to hear the strange sounds better. Another beat.)*

FERDINAND: It's gone.

BETHANY: Yes.

FERDINAND: I don't hear it anymore.

BETHANY: If the sink doesn't get fixed soon I'll never be able to clean his garments again.

(A long, silent moment between BETHANY *and* FERDINAND.*)*

BETHANY: He read your letter. And then he disappeared.

FERDINAND: I'm sorry.

BETHANY: All I have left now is the memory of him, reading your letter and calling my name out in rage—

(Off-stage sounds of a toilet flushing. This startles the both of them. Then, the noisy sounds of a door unlocking and opening. BETHANY *and* FERDINAND *stare at one another and gasp…Could it be possible? Another short, dramatic beat. Then,* MAN *walks onstage. He is wearing a long, black*

*coat and we are unable to see his hands since it looks like
he is hugging himself with his hands wrapped within the
folds of the coat.* He looks curiously at both BETHANY *and*
FERDINAND. *They are frozen, staring back at him. A beat.)*

MAN: Hello.

BETHANY: Hello.

FERDINAND: Hey.

(A beat)

MAN: *(Speaks with a slight accent)* Has everyone gone?

BETHANY: Yes. Are you alright?

MAN: What do you mean?

BETHANY: You were in the bathroom for a very long
time.

MAN: I was…lost.

BETHANY: Oh. Did you know my husband?

MAN: Yes. I came to pay my respects. *(To* BETHANY*)*
And you were his wife.

BETHANY: Yes.

MAN: Bethany.

BETHANY: Yes.

MAN: It's nice to finally meet you. You were crying so
much earlier, it made you a little unapproachable.

BETHANY: I know. I'm sorry.

MAN: *(Gracious)* Oh no…no need…well, it's an
unapproachable kind of day, isn't it? A husband
disappears; no one can quite explain why…still…
there's a reason for everything, yes? I know…he knew
it, too; your husband…He spoke of you. He spoke of
how every man who's ever gone through your kitchen
can never forget the fragrance that emanated from
your laundry…your sluicing…That the scent you

created was something so potent, so intoxicating... almost a siren's call for one's nostrils...and you always sluiced right over the kitchen sink, didn't you? Right over the disposal... *(Pointing to a few of the clothes; keen interest)* Have those been sluiced? Have they?

BETHANY: Some of them. Not all of them.

MAN: Aaah, I see. I see. May I take a little whiff?

FERDINAND: *(Jealously)* Hey! How did you know her husband? Who are you?

MAN: I was a close friend of the family.

FERDINAND: I'm a friend…

MAN: Yes, but…

FERDINAND: …And I don't remember ever seeing you before—

MAN: I understand that, but—

FERDINAND: *(To* BETHANY*)* Do you know this guy?

BETHANY: *(Shaking her head)* No.

MAN: *(To* BETHANY*; sighs deeply)* Your husband's people are the same as my own…we're of shepherd stock; from the farthest side of the Peninsula; a cluster of tiny villages clumsily situated between Hungary and Bulgaria. And I say 'clumsy' because…well, we never stay in one place for very long. It's our style; you see… we're known for our wild and roaming ways… *(Smile)* We're the kind of people who communicate with each other only by our thoughts…messages whispered into cinder boxes, or little hexes invoked from behind stained-glass window panes…we still believe in magic…we believe in such things as love potions, and witches' familiars, and protective talismans, oh, and of course, shape-shifters…!

BETHANY: Shape-shifters?

MAN: Yes. People who can change their physical forms at will. It's an old trick, you see and not a bad skill to have if one is traveling between Hungary and Bulgaria.

BETHANY: *(Fascinated)* How is that possible? I mean, what can these...people...turn into?

MAN: Oh, all sorts of things! There's really no limit... let me see now...well, some can turn themselves into small animals...while others can become any sort of inanimate object you can imagine—a table lamp, or perhaps a rocking chair...

(Noticing that FERDINAND is holding the pants and sniffing them again)

MAN: ...or even a pair of men's pants...

(FERDINAND immediately drops the pants in sudden horror)

MAN: There's really no limit. Some can even make themselves smaller...infinitely smaller... smaller to the point where they can easily slip into the teeniest and tiniest of places. Like a wedding ring. And they will stay there for as long as they like. Until they choose to come back out again.

(BETHANY and FERDINAND slowly look at one another and burst into a fit of nervous laughter. A beat)

FERDINAND: That's gotta be the most ridiculous thing I've ever heard.

MAN: *(To him)* Why is it so difficult to believe? If there are organisms, living things, creatures of breath and spleen, and blood that can disappear for long periods of time, only to one day return again, what makes you think anything is impossible? Nothing is impossible. *(A short beat)* Life is odd.

FERDINAND: *(Growing anger)* Bunk. It's all bunk. Who do you think you are?

BETHANY: *(Worriedly)* Ferdinand—

FERDINAND: Showing up here and telling these ridiculous tales—

BETHANY: Ferdinand—leave him alone!

(FERDINAND *roughly grabs* MAN *and pulls his arms apart.* MAN's *coat opens and we see that the front of his shirt is covered in blood. Both* BETHANY *and* FERDINAND *gasp out loud at the sight of this. A dramatic beat)*

MAN: *(Sheepish)* I'm sorry. I'm afraid I had a little accident in your bathroom.

BETHANY: *(Aghast)* Accident? You look like you've been mauled by a pack of hungry lions!

MAN: It's not so bad.

FERDINAND: Were you trying to kill yourself?

MAN: Probably.

BETHANY: Why?

MAN: I miss my wife. She's gone, you see…

FERDINAND: *(Sneering)* Did she shape-shift into a car and drive off?

BETHANY: Ferdinand!

MAN: *(Chuckles)* No, she didn't…but that's very funny…Jack always said you were funny. No, I thought she was leaving me for someone else and I didn't know what to do.

BETHANY: We have to call an ambulance.

MAN: No, no ambulance—
A man should marry for love, yes? I did.
And I loved her more than my own life.
But she was not one of my people. Or Jack's.
Perhaps this was a mistake on my part.

FERDINAND: Why?

MAN: Oh, she was an awfully curious woman. Very, *very* curious.

My people have always been wild nomads bordering the isthmus.

But we've never been... *(As though saying a "bad" word)*...curious.

But she...she was always reading. Always asking questions. Always going out during the day.
Not getting home until late.
It caused problems for us.
I became jealous; I accused her of terrible things. At times, I locked her up.
Finally, she stopped denying everything.

BETHANY: Did she admit to being unfaithful?

MAN: Oh, no. She just stopped talking. She simply refused to ever speak to me again. Not a single word.
It was unbearable.
Can you imagine what that felt like?
Being with another person, legally and fully, but having to be there completely in silence?
It made me feel helpless and weak. Fragile.
And a man should never feel fragile.
In the meantime, I still had no idea what she was doing. Out there.
Dear Lord, the thoughts that would come to me; the scenarios I had running through my head.
I knew I had to do something—

BETHANY: *(Excited at the thought)* So, you *turned*! You shape-shifted, didn't you?

MAN: That's right—
Every day, she'd leave our apartment
I'd be convinced she was off to see another man
And that's when I knew what I had to do
One day...right before she left again...I willed myself into her wallet

I WILLED MYSELF into her purse
(In rapture over the memory) Oh, her purse! I *loved* the
smells that came out of her purse!
The same way Jack loved the smells that came from all
your sluicing
Over the kitchen sink.
I managed to place myself right between her silver-
handled hair brush
And her double mint gum
And once I felt the velvet, silk lining against my skin, I
knew I'd done it…once I sensed the constant clink and
jangle of her coins, the coolness of the silver, hear her
cell phone ring, smell the sugary smoke and fresh, pure
mint of the chewing gum—
I knew I was in a paradise unmatched by any passage
found in the Bible.
It was a marvel.

FERDINAND: *(Shaking his head)* What nonsense—

BETHANY: *(Charmed)* Oh no. It sounds so romantic.

MAN: *(deeply moved by the memory)* Yes, it was. It truly
was. It was…romantic. Like a passionate dream I'd
never wake up from. I was closer to her in a way
that was thrilling and completely unlike a husband.
I was near her constantly, every single day, right up
against the side of her body where her purse bounced
deliciously up and down against her hip. *Oh, it was so
wonderful!*

BETHANY: Yes. Yes, it sounds wonderful—

MAN: But my most favorite thing was when she'd
suddenly open the bag and slip something inside…
(The memory is almost arousing) Oooh! It could be
anything; a new powder compact…a tube of lipstick…
or even a tiny container of Tic-Tacs! It was my favorite,
you see, because then, I might get to see her…I might
catch a glimpse of her face; a whiff of her perfume…I'd

feel the warmth coming off her tender fingers, feel her heart beating each time she'd hold the bag against her chest as she'd make change at the grocery store... Oh God—what a lovely woman!

BETHANY: How sweet.

MAN: After a while, I had no desire to leave. Why should I? It didn't matter how long I stayed inside; I was a man in love—I was happy!

FERDINAND: But what about her other lovers?

MAN: *There were no other lovers!* You see, that was the best part; I was wrong about her. She was never unfaithful to me. I WAS WRONG!

(The three of them share a triumphant moment together.)

BETHANY: So, it all worked out well...yes?

(A beat.)

MAN: I made a mistake.

I stayed too long...inside her purse...I...I stayed in there for years.

Without realizing it.

BETHANY: For years? How is that possible? I mean, didn't you ever get hungry?

MAN: No. The smells in her wondrous purse was all the food I needed.

FERDINAND: Wow.

MAN: It was all the sustenance I could want.

FERDINAND: But she thought you'd gone.

MAN: Precisely.
She thought I left her.
Because I'd been so jealous and angry, she thought I left.
(A beat) I didn't know.

I never realized
All that time, I didn't think about what my
disappearance was doing to her.
I was so happy, I could only think of myself.
I didn't know—
*(He can't go on with the story…there is a brief, heavy
silence.)*

FERDINAND: What happened to your wife?

MAN: *(After a pause)* She came home one night…
dropped her purse on top of the bed, just like she
always did…and she consumed a bottle of sleeping
pills.

BETHANY: Oh no!

FERDINAND: *(Moved)* Oh man—

MAN: I never would have known. I might have stayed
in there forever.

BETHANY: Your poor wife…!

MAN: Finally, it was Jack who coaxed me out. The
only way you can get someone to shift again is to
entice them. Persuade them. It was Jack who made me
realize, I had to come out.

BETHANY: But how did he do that? How would he
know—?

MAN: He sang me a song. My favorite song:
(He begins singing)
Somewhere beyond the sea,
Somewhere, waiting for me,
My lover stands on golden sands
And watches the ships that go sailing…
Once I heard him…once I started singing along with
him…that was it—I was out of the purse.

FERDINAND: *(Shaking his head; deeply moved by story.)*
Incredible.

MAN: I promised Jack I would do the same for him
If it ever came to that.
And so...one day...he reads a letter
It's a letter from his best friend
And in the letter the best friend says he's in love with
his wife.
And Jack...well...suddenly he has no idea what to
think.
No idea what to feel.
And I think he laughs a little at the thought of what
he's lost.
And all he can really think about is what he must have
done to turn both his wife and his friend
Against him.

BETHANY: (*To* FERDINAND; *desperate whisper*) He's
talking about your letter! *He knows!*

FERDINAND: (*Whispering as well*) But I don't
understand...how could he?

MAN: And he thinks to himself, "If I can be so cold and
blind in my heart...I am deserving of the darkness.
Then perhaps I must be in a place that is also cold and
blind.
Where nothing can be seen,
Nothing is felt, and it should probably be a little damp,
too, because I don't normally like damp things so I
ought to have myself in a damp and clammy place as
well."
He figures it will serve him right, yes?
And then, the next thing he knows
He turns...he *shifts*...he is in that exact, same place
Feeling the chill
Lost in the dark
Wishing it could've been different.
(*To* BETHANY) Your husband is near.

(The odd, teeny sound is suddenly heard again. They all hear it and turn towards the kitchen sink. The sound is heard again. A beat. They all slowly move towards the sink and bend their heads down towards it as though to hear the strange sounds better. The odd sound is heard again, and this startles them. A long, dramatic beat.)

BETHANY: Wait a minute… *(Growing horror; to* MAN*)* … are you saying that he's…he's…he's down…there…? *(Pointing)*

MAN: I've been in the same situation myself, you see—

BETHANY: Down there? *There?* How? How is that possible? How can he be…? In there? Down the drain? In there? Where is he, exactly? In the disposal? *(Becoming hysterical)* But…but…but…but…but… that's…that's not possible—

FERDINAND: *(Becoming distraught)* Jack was a large man…A BIG MAN…he couldn't just fit himself…down there…Why would he put himself down there?

BETHANY: Why would he do this? He can't…he can't be…*down there!* NOT DOWN THERE!

FERDINAND: *(Towards the sink)* Jack? Buddy, can you hear me?

MAN: I disappeared, but I came back…

BETHANY: Not down there!

FERDINAND: *(To* MAN*)* I think you should leave.

BETHANY: *(Still at the sink)* Not my husband!

MAN: I had a wife. My wife—

FERDINAND: *(To* MAN*)* Get out of here!

MAN: *(Still to* BETHANY*)* I thought she left me for someone else…but it wasn't true…!

BETHANY: *(Still at the sink)* Oh God…! I think I can smell his cologne!

FERDINAND: I think I smell it, too—

BETHANY: *(Pushing him away from the sink)* Get away from me! I don't want him to hear your voice!

FERDINAND: *(Pushing her back; like an angry child)* He was my friend, too!

MAN: I chose to come back. Perhaps Jack will feel the same way. *(To her)* Bethany?

BETHANY: Yes?

MAN: Would you like to see if you can bring him back?

BETHANY: *(Guiltily)* I can't.

MAN: Why not?

BETHANY: *(After a pause)* I'm an unfaithful wife.

(The MAN looks towards FERDINAND. He shakes his head, sadly.)

FERDINAND: *(Another beat)* I'm a disgrace as his best friend.

MAN: You both love him. You miss him. It may be enough. All you can do is ask.

FERDINAND: How can I help?

MAN: It needs to be something he would emotionally respond to—

BETHANY: That could be anything!

MAN: No. It has to be *specific*; like a song, a poem… something that would make him react. Pull him out of himself.

FERDINAND: I could tell a joke.

BETHANY: Ferdinand—please…

MAN: No. Wait a minute. That's a wonderful idea—

BETHANY: Excuse me?

MAN: Jack loves to laugh, remember? It would be a good way to get his attention.

BETHANY: Yes, but Ferdinand's not funny—

FERDINAND: *(Offended)* I'm funny—damnit!

MAN: You know that old saying 'two heads are better than one'? Perhaps the two of you can get Jack to shift…coax him out of the drain. Maybe you can tell jokes together.

FERDINAND: *(To* BETHANY*)* Can you follow my lead?

BETHANY: This is silly

MAN: *(A little stern)* Without faith, Bethany…it's all inconsequential.
Worthless. Unimportant.
Remember this.

(The odd, teeny sound is suddenly heard again. But the sound is different this time; sharper, a little louder, more ominous. This electrifies BETHANY, *who quickly hovers over the sink. The sound is heard again. It's louder.)*

BETHANY: Wait a minute…did you hear that? Did you? *(A beat; turns to* FERDINAND, *resigned)* Okay…what do you want me to do?

FERDINAND: I say something…you repeat it and then you respond…and then…I give you the punch line.

BETHANY: *(Hesitant)* All right.

FERDINAND: Ready? *(She nods)* Okay…here we go… *(Like a stand-up comic)*What is the last thing to go through the mind of a mosquito when it hits your windscreen?

BETHANY: What?

FERDINAND: *(Impatient)* Come on—

BETHANY: *(At a loss)* I don't understand the question!

MAN: *(kindly petulant)* My dear, it doesn't matter—

FERDINAND: Exactly. *It doesn't matter.* It's all about the delivery. *You* repeat what I've just said and then you respond to it. Okay? Let's try it again. "What is the last thing to go through the mind of a mosquito when it hits your windscreen?"

(BETHANY *looks at* FERDINAND *and the* MAN, *completely dumbfounded for a moment and then finally decides to 'go with it.'*)

BETHANY: I don't know. What is the last thing to go through the mind of a mosquito when it hits your windscreen?

FERDINAND: *(With a flourish)* It's ASS!

(A beat. Then, the three of them quickly lean over the sink. They listen. Nothing. FERDINAND *and* BETHANY *look towards the* MAN.)

FERDINAND: I don't hear anything.

MAN: Try again.

BETHANY: But—

MAN: How badly do you want him back? You can't give up after only the first try. Try it again.

FERDINAND: Okay. "When a man takes off his pants in a hotel room, what's the first thing to hang out?"

BETHANY: *(Starting to get 'into it')* I don't know, Ferdinand...when a man takes off his pants in a hotel room, what is the first thing to hang out?

FERDINAND: *(With a flourish)* "The DO NOT DISTURB sign!"

(Again, the three of them quickly lean over the sink. They listen. For a moment, there's nothing...and then...The teeny sound is heard again. Only this time, it's just a little bit louder...)

BETHANY: *(Overwhelmed)* Oh my God—

FERDINAND: *(Excitedly)* He's responding! *He's responding!*

BETHANY: *(To* MAN; *breathless)* Did you hear that? Did you? It sounded like him...I think it sounded like him—!

MAN: Yes, yes...it may be working. But you can't stop now. Keep going.

FERDINAND: *(Resolute)* Okay...Bethany, why don't people eat clowns?

BETHANY: *(Same energy)* Gee, I don't know, Ferdinand...Why don't people eat clowns?

FERDINAND: *(With the same flourish)* Because they taste *funny*!

(The MAN *laughs heartily at this one; we can see that* FERDINAND *and* BETHANY *are beginning to enjoy themselves. The teeny sound is heard again. It's working.)*

MAN: That's a good one.

FERDINAND: *(To* MAN*)* Thanks. *(To* BETHANY*)* "It was so hot in the city today..."

BETHANY: *(Over the sink; like a cajoling wife)* Honey...? Honey—can you hear me?

FERDINAND: *(Sharply)* Bethany!

BETHANY: *(To* FERDINAND; *distracted)* What?

FERDINAND: "It was so hot in the city today..."

(A beat. BETHANY *stares at* FERDINAND.*)*

BETHANY: *(Not sure how to respond)* "It was so hot in the city today...?"

FERDINAND: *(Shaking his head)* No. No. You need to respond by asking, "How hot was it?"

BETHANY: *(A beat)* That's not what you told me to say.

FERDINAND: *(Sharp)* But that's how you have to respond!

MAN: *(Mediating)* It's alright. It's all fine. It's working. Just start it again—

BETHANY: *(To* MAN*; miffed)* But that's not what he told me to say!

MAN: It doesn't matter.

FERDINAND: *(Exasperated; to* MAN*)* She's going to ruin it.

BETHANY: I am not—

FERDINAND: You have absolutely no sense of comic timing!

BETHANY: You're not being fair.

MAN: It's alright, Bethany. I'll do it with you this time, okay? We'll do it together.

FERDINAND: Okay. Are you ready?

(Both BETHANY *and the* MAN *nod;* FERDINAND *takes a moment to "prepare")*

"It was so hot in the city today..."

BETHANY & MAN: How hot was it?

FERDINAND: *(With a final and dramatic flourish)* It was so hot that we had to ask the Statue of Liberty to put her arm down...Phew! TALK ABOUT B-O!

(Both FERDINAND *and the* MAN *burst into laughter. Even* BETHANY *laughs in spite of herself. A jovial moment between all of them.)*

(But there's no sound coming up from the sink.)

(An abrupt anguished moment as they all stare down the sink.)

(And then...unexpectedly...another sound comes up through the drain. The sound is something between a gurgle and a titter beginning to rise up.)

(The three look at each other. They know what this means; Jack's laughing. They begin to laugh again as they continue to listen.)

(And as the gurgling sounds begin to escalate, so too does their laughter.)

(Slow blackout)

END OF PLAY